# CREATING CASH FLOW AND WEALTH THROUGH REAL ESTATE

*My First Five Houses*

Adam R. Albarado, DVM

# TABLE OF CONTENTS

# CHAPTER 1: STEPS AND HURDLES

This book is a no fluff, straight to the point, step by step guide how I attained my first five investment properties. It is intended to be an example for those just starting out what someone else has done to make it there. It is a template I wish I had when I began my journey to financial success. It also contains some tidbits on how my wife and I developed an early solid foundation that set us up for future success. This book focuses not only on the steps I took to purchase my first five investments properties, but also the mental hurdles and hesitations I had to overcome to make this positive change in my life. I hope this book can be relatable and a boost of confidence as I share my hesitations and fears as I pushed my boundaries.

This book is not intended to sell you anything. It is not meant to describe the intricate details of 401k's, roth ira's, investment strategies or anything else you can just search for on the internet. It is not a get rich quick scheme. It is not a path that lies before you to copy exactly, as we all have different life circumstances.

# CHAPTER 2: WHAT ARE THE RICH DOING?

I never had any doubt I would find a way to reach financial success. I knew there were rich people and poor people. All I had to do was what the rich were doing and I would become rich! Right? But wait, what were the rich doing? I had no idea. I knew some people invented things, some people started businesses, some people had lucrative jobs and became CEO's. Uh oh… road block. I did not know how to do any of those things. If only I could find out what the rich were doing, that I wasn't to become rich. I didn't know any rich people at that time. I grew up in a typical middle class neighborhood with friends that lived the same comfortable, but not rich, life style that I lived. Well, could I just find someone that is rich and ask them what they did? Hmmm… that's not that easy when you don't know any rich people, and even if I did, wouldn't that be kind of awkward? Nevertheless, I brainstormed often on how could I copy others. How could I just emulate what someone else did? Shouldn't I get the same results?

I didn't know how to start a business. I knew it had something to do with going downtown to a big building and forming an LLC… I think. But what about taxes?

What about a business license? Do I need an accountant or how about an attorney?

I didn't know how to get into real estate. Everyone said it was risky. I was told I'd be fixing toilets, dealing with non-paying tenants. I was told I should just get a steady good paying job and live comfortably. But, that wasn't for me!

Real estate provides a way to produce cash flow and increase net worth over time. But the uncertainty of investing in something outside of our comfort zone can be a daunting prospect. On the surface, investing in property can seem to be an expensive and risky venture. I know this, because I had many of the typical hurdles placed before me before I began my path to owning investment properties. I had no clue how it was done. I had no experience, I wasn't rich, and I had no team to help me along the way. Over time, I found ways over each of those hurdles, and now that those hurdles are behind me I have been able to enjoy the financial benefits of real estate investing. So, I would like to share my journey as I closed the deal on each of my first five investment properties. I will share my thoughts and fears through the process, and I will guide you step by step on the actions I took to change my thinking and go past my comfort zone.

# CHAPTER 3: ONLY TAKE ROCKET ADVICE FROM A ROCKET ENGINEER

When people begin their journey to financial freedom, the first people they usually ask advice from are their peers with similar life circumstances. Don't do this! You will likely be met with your first hurdle you placed in front of yourself. Everyone is quick to be a naysayer. And they are quicker to freely give out bad advice… horrible advice really. If you want to know how to make money, do not ask someone who is not making lots of money. If you want to know how to build a rocket you do not ask your peers. You instead go ask a rocket engineer! Knowledge and information are the most important foundations to your road to success. If you begin that road with a poor foundation, you'll never make it there. As well-meaning as your friends and family are, they can inadvertently crush your dreams with negativity and put you on the same path they are on to the daily rat race and paycheck to paycheck struggle.

I made this mistake. When I told friends and family I wanted to get into real estate, I was immediately met with resistance. I was told "I hope you like fixing toilets," "Then you have to deal with bad tenants," and I was even told, "You cannot make money in real estate." These responses came so quickly and effortlessly, it was clear that they were just repeating what they once heard from someone else. Perhaps their dreams were met with the same resistance, and their dream ended there?

Find the people who are already doing what you want to do. Speak to a high producing realtor with knowledge of your market. Connect with successful local landlords. There are a plethora of books and programs written and designed by successful real estate moguls. The knowledge they offer is a window into their world and possible path towards your successful future. These are your rocket engineers!

# CHAPTER 4: STEP 1, THE BEGINNING OF MY JOURNEY

So where did I get my initial information that formed a solid foundation? In college, my dad knew of my aspirations to become rich. My dad was visiting me at my dorm and handed me a book. He told me, "I would love to tell you how to make money, but I can't. I don't know how. Here is a book that I heard some good things about, so it will hopefully help you." He handed me the book, "Rich Dad, Poor Dad" by Robert Kiosaki. This was step one of my journey. My dad has always been there for me. When others would offer me bad advice and say things like, "You don't want to get into real estate. You don't want to deal with tenants. You don't want the responsibility of running a business. You want a steady job with benefits", my dad instead held his tongue. He may not have been able to give financial advice, but to know when to not give bad advice was one of his best gifts to me. Instead of bad advice he said nothing and let me dream. He then gave me a book written by a man that was successful and gave good advice. I say this was step one, because this was the first time I was able to communicate with a rich person. Sure, I couldn't ask him questions, but I could read Robert

Kiosaki's book. In it, I finally had a window into the mind of someone who had made it. On each page, I took in his words and felt like a light had been turned on. I reread that book three times. He was the rocket engineer, and I wanted to build a rocket! To this day, I highly recommend his books.

# CHAPTER 5: STEP 2, A SMART FINANCIAL START

I had just graduated college and so had my wife. We moved to another city to maximize our incomes in a booming area. We were each working and decided to build a strong financial foundation prior to having kids. We rented a small single bedroom apartment. It was cozy and met our needs. At that time in our lives we talked a lot about finances. We were aware of the ways of the world. We knew there were rich people and we knew there were poor people. We understood the hardship and struggles low income and poverty could cause. And at that time, the news was filled with stories of the widening wealth gap in our country that seemed to continue to accelerate. We pictured this as a bungee cord that would stretch in both directions with the rich on the right and the poor on the left. The far ends of the bungee cord were stretching faster from the middle than any other point. We knew we wanted to position ourselves as far to the right on the bungee cord as possible in this quickly changing world. To make matters worse, everything was getting more expensive and incomes across the board were not increasing at the same rate. To position ourselves for success, we needed a plan.

We decided we would only live off of the lesser income and the higher income would be saved. No matter what, we would not touch the income from the higher earner and it would be direct deposited into a savings account every two weeks. We pretended that the income did not even exist. Each month, it was a sense of pride to look into the savings account and see the progress we made. In only 3 years, we had $150,000 in that savings account.

During that time, we sacrificed a higher standard of living. We rarely ate out, we clipped coupons, and shopped sales. Our entertainment budget was minimal. We would rarely shop for non-essentials. We could have upgraded to a nicer apartment or purchased a house, but remained content in our one- bedroom apartment. After a while, saving money just became habit. We wouldn't think twice about passing up the newest electronics, expensive furniture, or a new car. It even became a sense of pride. Our frugal habits became a joy as we watched our savings quickly grow. It was often that we would tell each other how much we saved that day by passing up our favorite morning mocha, or getting gas at the cheaper gas station, or by buying generic.

Our cars were paid off and as long as they were safe, we resisted the temptation to buy a new car. We knew a new car would mean a chunk out of our savings if we paid cash or monthly payments. A new car would be a luxury and it was not something we needed. We did not want to make monthly payments every month on something that would only depreciate in value. We took joy discussing the amount we were saving every month by continuing to maintain our current cars.

Having a partner that can share in my goals was paramount. My wife supported us on just her income in those three years. She has never been as driven to make money as I am, but was just as willing to be frugal and make sacrifices as I was to give us the best start possible. That start had made all the difference.

# CHAPTER 6: OUR FIRST HOUSE (MY FIRST TASTE OF REAL ESTATE)

After three years of diligent saving, my wife wanted a house. I didn't. I was a bit scared of a mortgage. I loved socking away my entire income every two weeks, and watching our savings account grow. But this was something she really wanted and, in a marriage, or partnership, compromise is important. We found a master planned community with hundreds of houses. We bought the smallest house ($135,000) following the old adage to buy the cheapest house in the best neighborhood. The community had houses that went upwards to over $1,000,000. We wouldn't be throwing money away on rent anymore, and would be making principle every month not including the appreciation of the property. We put $50,000 down on the property and carried an $85,000 mortgage for 30 years fixed.

While living there, I realized that our pride of ownership never diminished. Whereas a purchase like a car is exciting and new for several months, sooner or later, it just becomes a mode of transportation. Its value drops as a depreciating asset. The same is true for most other purchases. But real estate is different.

Every day when I would drive home from work I would drive up to the house and have the pride of knowing I owned property! It was our home, and we both loved it. Whenever I would landscape the property or add an improvement, not only would I get the benefit of the completed task but I had a deeper sense of pride that I was improving the house and its value. Real estate was enriching my life financially and emotionally.

We took a very conservative approach to our property. Having a house to live in can be a wonderful asset but if treated incorrectly, it can be detrimental to your finances. When people purchase a house, often their first act is to fill that home with furniture and all those comforts of modern living. This is one of the reasons the housing market is such a strong indicator of how the economy is doing overall. When the economy is doing well, people are buying houses. When people buy a house, they fill it with things that they otherwise would not buy. And typically, it is only natural to fill the house. The bigger the house, the greater number of things that are purchased to fill the house. This can be a drain on savings and money for purchasing more assets.

We were careful to continue our diligent savings despite our new home. We purchased used furniture or bought during sales. We didn't let our new- found space fill with costly possessions. We continued to strengthen our financial foundation and our home truly was a financial and emotional asset.

# CHAPTER 7: STEP 3, NUDGED INTO REAL ESTATE INVESTING

A few years later, we decided to move to another state. I had an opportunity to buy a franchise from the business I worked for. The only problem, they were still building houses in the master planned community so we couldn't sell our house with brand new houses available to buyers. But we started look-ing for a house in our new city anyway because we could not afford to miss this opportunity, including a chance to be back in our home state. We found a new construction home in a new neighborhood. Our first house still had not sold so we were very hesitant to buy a second house. This was beyond our com-fort zone. My hesitations manifested as self-doubts. Was this a dumb decision? Would friends and family think we were irresponsible for purchasing a second house when our first hadn't sold yet? Would this eat into our savings? But I developed a plan. I thought back to Robert Kiosaki's book I read in college. I could rent my first house to continue to pay down the mortgage. And with a plan in place, after much deliberation and number crunching, we decided to take the leap.

Due to our continued diligent saving, we were able to place $100,000 down on the $218,000 house at our new location. And we were ready to rent our first property. If Robert Kiosaki could do it, so could I. My confidence was up. I couldn't wait to have my own rental property. Since it was in another state I would need a property management company to manage it for me. I went on the internet and found a company that would take care of everything including managing the tenants. I signed the contract with them. Their fee included the first month's rent, and $100 per month afterwards. I would be responsible for any maintenance and repairs on the property. This worked out well. Within a week, the property management company found our first tenant. The management company forwarded the contract signed by the tenant for me to sign and the deal was done. Our monthly payment on the house was about $1300 (with taxes and insurance) and the first renters were paying $1400 per month. Each month, our mortgage was payed for us and we continued to make principle and appreciation on the property.

Our new property was a bit scary. And as you'll see throughout this book, every step is scary if it pushes your boundaries. It was a $218,000 house and we would be carrying a $118,000 mortgage (30 year fixed). I never bought a house worth that much before. It was a big jump from the small $135,000 house I had before. I had lots of sleepless nights after signing the purchase contract. Did I make the right decision? Would this keep me from becoming rich? I couldn't sock away as much money every month with the larger mortgage. I had no one to tell me if I made a good decision. I only had my own mind trying to convince myself that I would still find a way to reach my dreams of becoming rich. The problem was, sometimes my insecurities would gain strength and I would question my future.

# CHAPTER 8: STEP 4, FAILURE

I purchased a franchise business in 2008. This was exactly at the time the real estate market and stock market crashed. It was a struggle at first. It seemed like every other client was out of work or had a spouse that lost their job. I was not making the money I wanted to make. Eventually the business did fine, but in the beginning I was depressed. I dreaded every month when I would get my profit and loss statement. Some months were ok, but other months I would struggle to put a smile on my face to not worry my wife. I was just learning how to manage a business so I made a lot of mistakes. At the time, I beat myself up for every mistake. I obsessed on those mistakes and my insecurities grew. I wish I could go back in time to tell myself it was ok. Those mistakes made me wiser, and I would not be who I am today without those mistakes. After all, why did I expect to be perfect at something I had never done before?

I had the chance to accept my income level, and to accept I would never be highly successful in business. But that wasn't for me. I had a wife and just recently had a son. I wanted them to have the life I pictured they deserved. I became angry. I would spend many nights lying on my son's bedroom floor at night as he fell asleep, staring at the ceiling questioning everything I was doing. I knew others in this world were becoming rich. So why couldn't I? Then one night, I had a realization. If I keep doing what I'm currently doing, then nothing will change. So the key was to do something different! It was foolish to think that I could keep doing what I do every day, and somehow things would suddenly change to my favor and then everything would be better. Sure, it's easy to tell ourselves... sometime soon it will all get better... in the future an opportunity may come my way. But I decided to be honest with myself, and that made all the difference. I was not on a path to become rich, and it was my choices that were causing it. I was letting my failures be failures, and not opportunities to learn and strengthen myself. I made a conscious effort, that I would change my actions, I would change my mindset, and I would push myself forward no matter the discomfort level. I let my failure drive me to become stronger. I knew I was going to be rich, and I just needed to take action! I thought back to "Rich Dad, Poor Dad." Why not real estate? That is how Robert Kiosaki made his start. If I emulate him, surely I could have similar results! I already had my prior house that was being rented, so I've already had a small taste of what real estate could offer.

A few nights later I was lying down on my son's bedroom floor staring at the ceiling fan as he fell asleep in his crib, I thought to myself, "I only have one life to live. Now is my chance. I cannot just continue to dream. I have to take action!" I thought back to many of the life quotes we all hear from time to time. "When life knocks you down, you need to get back up and keep pushing forward." That is what I would do. I would go for it! If I was going to fail, then I would fail going after something big! I would push my boundaries as I've never done before. I would purchase a second rental property. On the outside, I was pumped and confident, and on the inside, I was shaking like a leaf.

# CHAPTER 9: STEP 5, SPEAKING WITH MY WIFE

We all have multiple journeys. I have my financial journey and the wonderful journey of life with my family. I had to find a way to manage my responsibilities as a husband and father and to do that I needed the blessing of my wife. After my night of revelation, I went to my wife and told her "I want us to be rich. And if I keep doing what I'm doing now, we won't be. I need to do something different. I want to get into real estate. This is something I really want to do." My wife didn't hesitate. She said, "If it's really something you want to do, then do it. It seems that you have thought a lot about it." I felt like a weight was lifted from my shoulders, as I did not know prior how she would respond. A huge potential hurdle was moved from my path, and my wife would walk that path with me. This was paramount to meeting my responsibilities at home and continuing on my journey to become rich.

My wife has been incredibly supportive in my ventures. From my days as a franchise owner to owning multiple properties, she has always trusted my decisions. Without her approval and agreement, I could not have attained my current level of success. Because of her, I was able to push my boundaries with support at home.

# CHAPTER 10: STEP 6, EDUCATION AND FACT FINDING

I had an idea. Now I needed a plan. And to make a plan, I had questions that needed answering. I needed to surround myself with a team. If I wanted to buy a house, I would need a down payment and a mortgage. But I wasn't a seasoned investor. Would I look like a fool? Here I am, another person that wants to get into real estate. Would the bankers treat me as a joke, as someone that is a fool getting in over his head, or perhaps a young kid that's just wasting their time? At that point, it didn't matter. I was angry I wasn't becoming rich. I decided to push my comfort zone and get my questions answered for I had made a commitment on my future!

I went to the bank and asked to speak with a manager about possibly getting a loan. They were very polite, and told me to sit in the lobby and she would be with me shortly. Her name was Melba. When she came out to speak with me, I had been rehearsing my questions in my head over and over. Her calm demeaner put me at ease. I introduced myself and we went into her office. After I sat down she asked me, "So what brings you in today?" I was very blunt. I asked, "I want to get into real estate and rent houses. What are my options to get a loan? Ideally, I would prefer to not use any of my money." To my instant relief, she said "Sure, let's see what we can do." What's this? They were taking me seriously and were respectful. It was not at all like some of the less than ideal scenarios I had invented in my head. We discussed several options, one of which sounded perfect. Since I had $100,000 principle in my home I could take out a home equity line of credit (HELOC). I could take out as much as $80,000 and could use that money to fund any down payments and improvements on a property. They could then get me in touch with the mortgage department to get pre- approved for a loan. Yes! I no longer had to wonder how to get started. My confidence was growing. I could already see the benefit to our strong financial foundation we formed with our early days of sacrifice and savings. Next, I needed a realtor. I contacted my realtor Scott, who sold us our house and happened to be one of the best realtors in the state. Again, he was another rocket engineer who had the know-how. He has a wealth of information to offer and through our initial conversation I found out he had rental properties of his own. The pieces of the puzzle were fitting together. I told him I did not want to be a slum lord. I wanted to purchase single- family middle-class homes worth at least $100,000 that could attract good tenants. And the timing was right. Due to the market crash, the housing market was a buyer's market with many foreclosures to choose from and low interest rates. The down turn in the market, became an opportunity.

At this time, I began reading all the information I could find on managing rental properties. I scoured Zillow.com to learn our city and current rental rates. I checked the city website and found a wealth of information of laws governing landlords and tenants. I also read books on real estate investing, and learned more about mortgage types, amortization schedules, and tax implications of rental properties. I also researched the legal implications of real estate and what I should have and not have in my lease agreements. Each item I would learn about would often branch in to other topics and create even more questions for me to research. I was becoming more confident in my knowledge base for real estate investing.

# CHAPTER 11: MY TEAM WAS COMING TOGETHER

My team was already coming together. I had a banker, a mortgage lender, and a realtor. Later, my team would grow and change. I would pick a handyman, a plumber, an air conditioner repairman, a roofer, pest control company, inspector, an accountant, a financial manager, and others. It was amazing how naturally and effortlessly my team came together once it was started. Much of the team did not know each other, but all were paramount to my success. It was my rocket engineer team!

A misconception that I had early on was that I would be a bother to others or my questions would bore them. To the contrary, I have found that people love to share their knowledge. It is wonderful to feel useful to others, and my entire team have always been quick to answer my questions and share their vast experience. In the beginning I had very little knowledge about investing in real estate, but it was ok because my team had the knowledge for me as I learned!

# CHAPTER 12: STEP 7, TIME FOR SOME MATH

If I was going to do this, I needed to be smart about it. I knew that I needed to find a good house in a good area with a good price. But what was a good price? I needed to find out the going rent in the area. I used various resources including Zillow.com and my realtor to determine average rental prices in the area. I came up with $1200 per month for the type of home I wanted in the areas I wanted. Ok... so if I can collect $1200 per month, I need the property to cost substantially less than that for me to make a profit. So, if I were to buy a $100,000 house and put 20% down with my home equity line of credit (HELOC), then what would my payment be? Here is my calculation I used:

Monthly payment for HELOC + Monthly payment on $80,000 mortgage (30 year fixed at 5% interest rate) + insurance + (flood insurance /12)= total payment

And then...

Monthly income − Total payment − any repairs and maintenance fees = PROFIT

On top of that, every month my mortgage payments would produce principle. And I averaged that over time, the typical property appreciates at 3% per year which would increase the value of the property by about $3000 yearly.

And I could depreciate the property, further reducing my tax burden.

It was time for my first concrete actions. I filled out an application for a HELOC loan. Very soon after, I found out that the application was approved and I had $80,000 of other people's money ready to use. I then went to my mortgage lender and filled out an application for a mortgage and received my pre-approval letter three days later. I was ready, motivated, and scared out of my mind.

# CHAPTER 13: LATE FOR THE PARTY?

Had the time for real estate investing come to pass and I missed it?

As I was about to delve head first into real estate. I kept having a nagging thought. How could I compete with the big dogs? I had seen the commercials and advertisements for companies that will pay cash for houses, tv shows dedicated to flipping houses, and I was familiar the names of those that became rich in the 70's investing in real estate. It was 2011 so surely, I missed the opportunity. Robert Kiosaki and others had their books out and many courses were available on real estate so others with more knowledge and influence than myself were most assuredly already out there gobbling up all of the best properties. Right?

Wrong. Throughout the United States there are millions and millions of people and thousands and thousands of cities. Our population continues to grow and more houses are built all the time. Real Estate is a constant ebb and flow of buying and selling. And the lives of the people that own the houses are in a constant flux of having kids, marrying, divorcing, moving, getting layed off, retiring, and dying. There is always change. And change brings new opportunities. For the big dogs in real estate, even they are in a constant flux of buying, selling, retiring, and periods of growing capital. There are always opportunities in real estate for it is intimately tied to the ever-changing circumstances of real people's lives. As you drive down the road, look out the window at all the new homes being built, for sale signs, for lease signs, new business development, and even garage sales. These are all part of the organic flow of peoples' lives and is evidence of continual change that bring opportunities to the market.

There will also be down turns in the market. These are opportunities to buy distressed housing including foreclosures. And when the market is suppressed, interest rates are generally lowered by the government to stimulate housing. On the flip side, when markets are up, interest rates are higher and properties are more expensive. This persuades some potential buyers to rent instead of buying. The ebb and flow of the real estate market continually provides opportunities on both sides of the coin.

# CHAPTER 14: STEP 8, THE BIG LEAP- PURCHASING A PROPERTY

I called my real estate agent and told him I was ready. I had my pre- approval letter from the mortgage lender to show sellers I meant business. I gave him a list of my criteria. I was looking for a three or four-bedroom typical middle class home worth at least $100,000 that I could possibly purchase for less than $100,000. It had to be in an area with increasing property values with easy access to the main roads. He created a list of properties that fit my criteria and he drove me around to tour the properties. Some of the properties I viewed were a disappointment. Many had major issues, that I was not yet comfortable addressing such as foundation issues, severely outdated kitchens and bathrooms, and severe damage from years of neglect. Was this all that was available? Did they all really require so much work? They just did not fit into my pre-imagined perfect rental home. It was a hit to my motivation and excitement. My realtor assured me that it was ok. He told me it was just part of the process. We would continue to look at properties until we found the one that just feels right. And he was correct! After viewing several more properties with my real estate agent, I found one that would be perfect. It was a four-bedroom, two bath single story. It was a foreclosure selling below market value. The bank that owned the property had already painted it and put in fresh carpet. It was in a typical middle-class neighborhood, was close to interstate with easy access to many businesses. It was not far from where I lived so it would be easy to manage.

There were only minor repairs and improvements needed. Scott was very knowledgeable and was able to help me estimate the costs of minor improvements that were needed. We walked the property and by the end, I knew I would have to spend about $3000 after the purchase of the property to get it ready to lease.

My realtor and I were standing in the driveway. The property just felt right. From my research and Scott's comparisons of surrounding properties, I knew I could rent it for $1200 per month and with my payments I could make substantial profit every month. I thought to myself, this is it, but there was a slight hesitation. Was I really doing this? Was I really about to buy an investment property? Could it fail and everything was about to come tumbling down? No! I reminded myself that if I do not change what I am doing then nothing will change! I have to take the next step. I have to act. I did the math, and I did the research. I had my team. I told Scott, "I want to buy this property. This is the one." He said "Great, I'll get the paperwork together and we will give them an offer." And at that moment I had moved out of my comfort zone and it felt great. It felt like living!

Later that day, he had an offer letter ready for me to sign. I signed it and he sent it to the bank that owned the property. I had to wait three days and they made a counter offer. I accepted.

I put an offer and eventually purchased the property in August, 2011 for

$87, 912 at 5%. My realtor walked me through the entire process. At the time, based on price comparisons Scott put together for me, we estimated its true market value to be ~$120,000. I utilized my HELOC to put 20% down and financed the rest. I used $0 of my own money. I spent several thousand dollars on improvement from the HELOC account.

Back to the calculations:

Monthly payement for HELOC ($150) + Monthly payment on mortgage ($377) + taxes and insurance($140) + flood insurance ($50)+HOA fees ($0) = Total monthly payment $717

Monthly rental income ($1200) − Total monthly payment ($717)= $483 monthly profit!!

I was scared but repeatedly reminded myself that the math doesn't lie. Even if I was way off on the rent and only rented it for $1000 per month I would still make $333 per month profit not including principle and appreciation.

After I purchased the property, I found a handyman named Bill that someone at my work recommended. We walked the property and he helped me make minor improvements over the next few weeks.

I was excited and wanted to do everything right. I would frequently stop by the property on my way to work in the mornings to go over my checklists and evaluate the repairs. Also, it was just fun and exciting to know that I owned that piece of property. I would enjoy walking through the rooms knowing that I finally took a big step towards my future.

One evening while repairs were still being completed, I went online to buy some direction signs that said "House for Lease" and had my phone number on them. The signs were around $40. Back then, it was hard to spend that $40 because I was way outside my comfort zone and had not seen even one dollar of rent yet. It felt like another $40 in the hole. I had to keep telling myself in the big scheme of things $40 is not much and I'm doing big things now. Rich people do not concern themselves with trivial amounts. I needed to think of money differently. I needed to think like a rich person. I wish I could go back to that night and tell myself not to sweat it. As later, my mindset has changed and I would not think twice about making a $40 investment. I listed the property on craigslist and Zillow.com. People began calling me almost immediately.

I set up times for people to view the property. I had no idea what to say when they showed up, so I just offered to tell them the basics of the house, the rent amount, and gave them a tour. I handed everyone a rental application form Scott was nice enough to give me. He also gave me a lease contract that he used on his properties for when I picked a tenant. After gathering a lot of applications, I reviewed them and picked a tenant that could afford the property and seemed courteous and polite during our first meeting.

They agreed to meet at the house. I offered either a one year or two year lease agreement. The rent for one year would be $1250 per month, and if they signed for two years the rent would be $1200 per month. They signed the contract for a two year lease. They gave me $1200 deposit and $1200 for the first month's rent. When they handed me the cashier's check, I felt a wave of relief. I couldn't believe I just got my first tenants in a house I intentionally bought to use as an investment. My confidence was at an all- time high.

My second surge in confidence came one month later. My tenants showed up on time and handed me the next month's rent of $1200. I did it! I changed what I was doing, took concrete actions, and I saw the rewards for my efforts.

It is now 2023, the market has recovered, and the property's estimated value is $190,000 and it is rented at $1,400 per month. The estimated value is $102,088 more than the purchase price. That is a $102,088 return from putting down $0 of my own money!

# CHAPTER 15: STEP 9: RINSE, WASH, REPEAT

I only had my first intentional investment property for about 2 months, when I decided to purchase another property. I had some fear, but nothing like before. Much of that fear had been replaced with confidence driven by my new gained knowledge. I had opened a checking account for my real estate venture and I watched every month as the money coming in was greater than the money going out. I still had plenty of money available in my HELOC account so I copied the same steps as before and bought my third investment property. It was another foreclosure, and was a three- bedroom two bath house. I purchased it for $105,000 in October of 2011. Its estimated market value was $130,000. It soon had a tenant. Today, that same property is valued at $185,000. That is an $80,000 return on putting down $0 of my own money. Today, this property rents for $1300 per month. Keep in mind, that these returns do not take in affect the principle that is being paid down by the tenants making their monthly rental payments. After purchasing this property, I had a total of two investment properties intentionally purchased to rent. In addition, I had my previous out of state house being managed by a property management company as a rental. It was at this time that I realized that with more properties it was not getting harder, it was getting easier. At this time, if I needed to pay for repairs or maintenance on one of the properties, there was more income coming in every month to utilize as opposed to using my HELOC account. And due to the increase in my net worth and monthly income, it was becoming easier to qualify for loans.

This process and transaction were almost effortless as I had just been through the process before. It was fun! I may not have truly been a seasoned investor but I felt like one. I knew what I was doing and I loved doing it. I couldn't wait to buy my next property!

Six months later I contacted my mortgage lender. At this time, I realized that the process was becoming more automated. My lender already knew me and my financial situation. Just a few quick financial updates was all that she needed to give me my next pre-approval letter. I called up Scott. I told him I got another pre-approval letter and I was ready for another property. This time he found me a house just hitting the market. It was not a foreclosure, but the owners were looking to sell it in a hurry. It was perfect. It was a four-bedroom, two bath home with a large yard. The back yard had a beautiful Japanese plum tree, fig trees, and citrus trees. There were two nice large sheds in the back. While I was walking the property with Scott I realized this would be my next property. I also realized another reason I loved buying property so much. This was a beautiful lot and house. It seemed like more than just an investment. It would be a tenant's home and I could take pride in providing such a beautiful house for someone. Real estate was giving me financial security, enjoyment, and pride. I purchased the property for $94,000. We estimated its value to be approximately

$130,000. I rented this property for $1300. Today, that same property rents for $1550 and is valued at $210,000. That is a $116,000 return on putting down $0 of my own money.

At this time, I made a big mistake. It was almost two years until my next property. To this day, I am not sure why I waited so long. I wish I would have continued purchasing properties during that time frame. I think I had become content. I was feeling somewhat successful and lacked the same hunger that drove my initial dive into real estate. But now I look back and wonder how much further ahead I could be if I continued with the same ferocity as the first few properties.

But after two years, I came to realize, that I was growing stagnant again. I was not achieving as much wealth as I was capable of achieving. I called up my mortgage lender and attained another pre-approval loan and sent my realtor on the look-out for another property. He found another foreclosure for me to look at. And by coincidence, it happened to be next door to my first investment property. It was a three-bedroom two bath house. I purchased the property for $107,500. It rented for $1300 per month. The property is currently valued at $200,000. That is a $92,500 return on putting down $0 of my own money. This property now rents for $1,750 per month. It was good to be in the real estate game again. At that time, I decided I would not make the same mistake twice. I would continue purchasing rental properties. I learned from my mistake.

# CHAPTER 16: CREATIVE FINANCING

On my fifth investment property purchase, I elected to use creative financing. For various reasons, I elected to not use a HELOC to finance a down payment, and as always, I prefer to use other people's money to make these investments instead of tying up my own funds. I also wanted to push my boundaries again and purchase a more expensive home over $200,000 that was newly built.

To finance the down payment on this next property I decided to do cash out refinancing on two of my existing rental properties. When I refinanced these properties, I elected to get a 15 year fixed loan on both of them! So in only 15 years or sooner if I pay down the principle, both of these properties will be paid for complete and clear. One of them is a property that is currently valued at $210,000 (I paid $94,000 by the way). Due to appreciation and the large amount of equity readily available, I was able to refinance the property to a 15 year loan and obtain a cash out refinance of

$50,000. It increased the mortgage payment from $700 per month to $1300 per month. My monthly rental income on the property is $1500 per month. So my profit on this property is now $200. I then cash out refinanced another property that is now worth $200,000 and took out $50.000 cash. I also refinanced this one as a 15 year mortgage so this property will also be payed for by the time I am 52 years old. It increased the mortgage payment from $700 to about $1300 per month and I currently collect $1750 per month on this property leaving me with $450 monthly profit.

However, since they are both 15 year loans the principle payments on both are substantial. $613 of the mortgage payment on the first property goes to principle every month and $512 of the mortgage on the second property goes to principle every month. And this does not include the benefit that these properties will continue to appreciate and the rent will continue to increase into the future.

So after refinancing these two properties, I had $100,000 cash to make as a down payment on another property. I decided to purchase new construction. While a builder is continuing to build in a neighborhood, generally, prices are suppressed. The builder wants to sell houses fast so the prices are generally reasonable. Also, with new homes being built, prices will not likely increase, as people will prefer to buy a brand new construction home as opposed to one that already had someone living in it. With a little patience, however; eventually the builder will move out of the neighborhood and prices can once again move with the market. With Scott's guidance, I purchased a new construction home for $223,505 and I put the entire $100,000 as down payment, leaving me with a 30 year fixed mortgage of $123,505 resulting in a monthly payment of $880. Due to the property's higher value and being new construction it is leased at $2150 per month, giving me $1,270 profit per month. This makes up for the reduced profit caused by refinancing the other two properties. And as of 2023, this property is now valued at $280,000. But now I have control over this additional property and will continue to benefit with the $170 currently going to principle every month from the mortgage payments, not excluding the greater appreciation a more valuable property will have. If the property attains a 3% increase in value per year, this will add over $6000 to the equity yearly. It is also another property that I can enjoy its tax benefits as the property is depreciated.

Over time, these benefits add up quickly. If you add the estimated value of my first five rental properties the total comes to $1,055,000. The total equity within these properties is about $493,000. My total principle earned monthly on those properties through the mortgage payments is ~$2000 per month. If those properties increase at an annual rate of 3% per year, that amounts to an additional $31,650 per year in equity just from appreciation. So, $2000 per month in principle +$31,650 from appreciation comes to a total increase in net worth of $55,650 per year not including cash flow and tax benefits from only 5 properties! Add in the approximately $2,100 of positive cash flow per month of those 5 properties and the total is $80,850 per year increase in net worth!!

# CHAPTER 17: SELLING MY FIRST HOME

Real estate investing can be very profitable and enjoyable, but from time to time, I really can see just how true this statement is. Due to some improvements that I needed to make for my franchise, I decided to sell my first home. For the purposes of this book, I did not consider it one of my first five investment houses since it was not intentionally purchased with the goal of leasing it. At the time of sale, the builder was finished selling houses in the neighborhood so prices were no longer suppressed and the market in general had improved. If you remember, I initially purchased the property for $135,000. That was in 2005. We sold it in 2015 for $185,000 which is a difference of $50,000. If you calculate a 3% increase in the property's value yearly for ten years, that comes to approximately $181,000 which is nearly right on with the selling price in 2015. The total interest that was paid on that property through the mortgage payments over that period of time, came to about $50,000 so we got back all that interest. And during the time we owned that property, we had paid down about $13,000 in principle which was reflected as an additional $13,000 we took home after selling.

You can see through this scenario the benefits of real estate. For most of the time we owned the property our tenants paid our mortgage plus some. The mortgage payments included principle every month which we got back at the time of the sale. And since we controlled the property, every year we were able to deduct the interest paid on the property through our taxes. And due to the appreciation of the property, we essentially got back all the interest we paid while owning it.

To this day, I wish I still owned this property. It had sentimental value to us being our first home. I also think of the continued cash flow I could still receive had I not sold it. It's current value with continued appreciation is approximately $300,000. And with today's market, this house would lease conservatively for $2,200 per month.

# CHAPTER 18: DETERMINING RENT

For each house, with Scott's help, I have strategically priced the rent. With his experience, he was able to estimate the rent that each property could produce. I would also look online on sites such as Zillow.com to determine what rent other people in the surrounding area were asking for similar houses. My goal has always been to get as much rent as possible for the current market conditions, but also to rent the property as quickly as possible. I would much prefer to take a slightly lower rent if it means having a tenant in the property. Even if a property is vacant just for a short amount of time while awaiting higher rent this could cause a significant loss. For example, if I have a property that based on all estimates should rent for $1300 per month, I first check the surrounding similar available properties for rent. I determine if the rent I am asking is competitive. If I can quickly obtain a tenant for $1300 per month rent then great. But if I hold out just two months waiting for a tenant willing to pay $1300 per month, then I have lost two whole months rent and have had to pay the mortgage payments out of my own pocket not including the electric bill and water bill. If, instead, I quickly rent the property for $1200 per month, I immediately have cash flow. With the preceding scenario even if I ultimately obtain the $1300 per month, it would take twenty-four months (two years!) to make up for the additional $2400 rent I could have made renting it for $1200 per month. I purchase rental properties for tenants and cash flow, not for holding vacant.

Also, having an unoccupied property opens a host of other issues including the possibility of vandalism, unseen weather damages, pests, etc. By pricing appropriately and fairly, the vacant periods can be kept to a minimum.

# CHAPTER 19: TODAY'S DOLLARS

When you purchase a property with a mortgage the total of the interest and principle payment stays the same month after month, year after year. As we are all well aware, it seems that there is always inflation. So, if your mortgage payment when you purchase a property is $800 before taxes and insurance it will be the same 20 years from now on a 30 year note. In 20 years, $800 will be worth much less than it is today. So over time, as our incomes increase and as the rent on properties continue to increase, the mortgage payment actually becomes easier and easier to make since it does not change! The payments throughout the entire course of the loan will be payments that you decided that you can pay in today's dollars. In the future those payments will be even less of a burden.

Some landlords do not care if they ever pay off a property. Of the five properties I listed, three of them have been refinanced to 15 year loans and two are 30 year loans. I structured it this way to help plan for an early retirement. The 30 year loans have lower mortgage payments so they provide a bulk of the positive cash flow. The 15 year loans have less cash flow but have the benefit of being paid in full when I am

52 years old. Then I will only need to pay taxes and insurance on the properties, and will have an additional $2,900 positive cash flow per month coming in just from these five properties. And this calculation is based on today's rental rates which will likely be much higher in the future. And at any time, I could take the monthly profits from these properties to pay down the principle even quicker resulting in even more cash flow once the properties are paid in full.

# CHAPTER 20: TIME

One of my initial hesitations of getting into real estate was the perceived length of time it would take to realize the fruits of my labor. I wanted to be rich but I did not want to wait until I was 65. As I discussed in prior chapters, from the purchase of your first property, you can begin to see the fruits of your labor with cash flow. Each additional property accelerates your progress more and more. In a short time frame the results can be substantial. However, real estate is not a get rich quick scheme. It takes work, dedication, and patience.

For the last one (patience), I am one of the least patient people I know. I can tell you that I like instant results. But as noted in the next chapter, I was the kid that also understood delayed gratification. From 2011 to 2019 I have done the work and I am already enjoying the fruits of my labor.

Being someone that has struggled with patience, the only other bit of advice I can give you, is that the time does pass. I cannot believe it has already been 8 years since my first rental property. It seemed like forever until I received my second month's rent on my first property. Back in 2011 looking ahead 8 years seemed almost pointless and frustrating. However, here I am, typing this book in 2019. The time did pass and I am glad that my past self was kind enough to provide for my future self. To this day, I regret that I did not invest in real estate even sooner. Take a moment and think of a time ten years ago. At that point, could you imagine yourself ten years into the future or was that too far away? Well, that time did pass and here you are ten years later. And another ten years will pass again.

Whether or not you have the foresight to see your successful future self, take the steps needed now because that time will come and your future self will thank you for it.

# CHAPTER 21: CONTROL OVER PROPERTIES

Purchasing a property lends a great deal of pride and satisfaction. When purchasing a rental property with a mortgage, you are utilizing other people's money to make your dream and investment a reality. Even though you may not have put a penny of your own money into the property you now have control over it. You decide whether to rent it or sell it. You decide how much rent to ask. You also reap the benefits. It may be the bank's money that purchases the house and the tenant's money that pays the mortgage but there are several other advantages to having the control.

First, there is the positive cash flow which can continue for as long as you own the home. This cash flow can be used to pay down the principle faster, it can be invested into improvements, it can pay for repairs, or it can be used for every-day living expenses.

Every single mortgage payment that is paid on the property has a portion of the payment that goes to principle. This is money that adds to your net worth. And with every monthly payment, the percentage that goes to principle increases. This principle can eventually be a source of cash-out refinancing for other properties.

In addition to the monthly principle, on average, properties appreciate in value which is added principle in the property. A general rule of thumb that a lot of people use is 3% appreciation per year. And the real estate market is no stranger to large price fluctuations including the possibility that prices could go down. However, historically they always come up again for most areas. And when they do go down; well, that is just another buying opportunity!

With control over the property, you get the added tax benefits. The current tax code allows for depreciation which can significantly reduce your tax burden. (Please check with your accountant as the details of depreciation are beyond the scope of this book) As you purchase your second property, third property, and so on you will find that it gets easier with additional properties. With the added cash flow, it becomes easier to make repairs and renovations further improving your properties' value.

# CHAPTER 22: LUCKY CHARMS

At this point, your first thought may be that this seems like a lot of work. And it is! But only in the beginning. It is the reward of delayed gratification that makes it all worth it.

When I was a kid, I knew the benefits of delayed gratification. When I would sit down to watch Saturday morning cartoons with my bowl of Lucky Charms it was really the marshmallows I wanted. So, I would eat only the cereal bits first. It wasn't that good, but I knew afterwards it would be worth it. By the end of the first cartoon, I had an entire bowl of only milk and marshmallows! And I could enjoy every single bite to the end of my shows with only sugary marshmallows. It was worth every bite of the cereal bits in the beginning.

Most people work 40 hours per week or more from about the age of 20 to 65 or longer. Day in, day out, living paycheck to paycheck they go through their lives. Their work never stops until retirement if they ever retire! On my first property I was making $483 per month profit every month not including principle and appreciation. How long does it take for the average person to earn $483 at their 9-5 job? So, I ask, what is more difficult? Working day in and day out to obtain

$483, just to have to do it again and again to continue earnings? Or is it better to obtain a loan, select a property, making an offer, and fill out mounds of paperwork just to get to the point where you can meet potential tenants to select a final applicant for

$483 profit? Well if it ended it there, it would be an easy decision, but once the house is purchased the hard work is over. That $483 per month will come again and again month after month for as long as you own the property. You will continue to gain principle. The property will continue to appreciate. The rent will likely go up with time earning you more and more with very little work. You've already eaten the cereal…now you get the marshmallows every month again and again!

# CHAPTER 23: IT'S GOOD TO FAIL

Most people want to avoid failure at all costs. But as the old saying goes, "Show me someone who has never failed, and I will show you a man who has never attempted anything." Success is a road with many stops at failure along the way. It wasn't until my franchise got off to a slow start that motivated me to dive head first into real estate. I've also made some mistakes in real estate along the way. I have paid too much for repairs. I have made too many improvements that were not needed to one property.

One particular failure I had was a property flip. I purchased the property with the intent to improve it, resell it and make a profit. I put in a lot of work. From finding the property, to purchasing the property, to the many trips to the property to manage the repairs, I remained a part of the process. However, I did not have enough room in my calculations for the unexpected. I did flip the property, but for only $1,800 profit when everything was said and done.

It was that particular failure that I took as a lesson. It would have been easier for me to make $1,800 at a 9-5 job then the amount of work and effort I put into that renovation.

Because of the property, I am now wiser. I have learned the importance of more planning for the unexpected, and more importantly I have learned what not to do. I realized that the time and effort to flip a property was not for me. After the sale, I would never see a penny again from that property. Whereas, with rental properties, the cash comes in month after month after month. The property continues to appreciate and I continue to have the pride of property ownership. Sometimes learning what you do not want to do is as important as learning what you do want to do. It is not to say that flipping properties is a bad thing, but in my experience, it is a lot of work for a one-time payout. Unless the payout is calculated to be substantial, I would prefer to rent my properties. Prior to this flip, another property I flipped netted me $10,000 so I considered that a successful flip. However, it too was a lot of work and since that day I have not seen another penny from that property!

# CHAPTER 24: 401K'S

Like many people I have a 401k. Beginning with my first job I maxed it out most years. As I've gained more experience I've come to realize that a 401k will provide a bit of security, but it is not something I can tap into until I'm 59.5 years old. I don't know about you, but I do not want to wait until I'm almost 60 to begin enjoying my riches and retirement.

4% is the typical amount most people recommend drawing from a 401k once you are 59.5 years old. Will this be enough cash flow to support your retirement?

Real estate can provide that added cash flow further diversifying your portfolio. A 401k is at the whims of the stock market and politics but in general, real estate usually goes up year after year. They aren't making any more land and we're at nearly 7 billion people on Earth. People will always need a place to live. And if the real estate market does drop temporarily that means foreclosures. This is buying opportunity and any one foreclosed will likely need a place to rent to live. Real estate leasing provides a valuable service to the community and that it is why the tax laws are generous to real estate investments.

I still contribute to a 401k, but only enough to get the full company match. I would rather invest in real estate and see that positive cash flow now!.. Not when I'm 59.5. Now that I'm 43 years old I am content with my 401k savings but I wish I would have instead placed more of that money into real estate.

# CHAPTER 25: HAPPINESS

You are likely reading this book because you are looking to make a change. Perhaps you are not happy with your current financial situation. Perhaps, you are unhappy in general. Perhaps money is the key to change that?

There has always been a lot of controversy and opposing opinions on what makes us happy. Researchers have studied relationships, income, social status and all types of underlying influences that drive our happiness. Does money make us happy? On one side of the discussion is the statement "Money is the root of all evil." Well, you can guess what side of the argument the people that use that phrase stand. You may have also heard "Money does not buy happiness."

The first statement is shrouded in shades of gray and the second statement has hints of truth in it. Sure, money can breed corruption. However, it is a lack of money (poverty) that often leads to drugs, abuse, and crime. Many of society's troubles and inequality is caused directly by a lack of money. Money in and of itself is not evil. Money made providing homes for families, improving houses which improve communities and property values, and money made to support your family is quite the opposite of evil.

For the statement that "Money does not buy happiness", it is partially true. But have you tried going without money. Not having money, can sure make you unhappy. It is the lack of money, that can lead to many types of stress in our lives and even depression. Money may not directly buy happiness, but it gives you a freedom... a freedom to spend more time with your family, a freedom to not have to worry about your family's financial security, and a freedom to now have to worry about the basic needs of your family; and that sure does make me happy knowing that I can provide this for them.

As I type a book based on making money and the importance of money, I continually remind myself, family is still most important. When a family member becomes sick, other than the finances needed to support their medical bills, you quickly realize that money means nothing in comparison to your loved ones. As long as we always remember that, it helps to keep our money-making ventures in context in the grand scheme sharing our lives with our loved ones.

Johnny Cash once said, "Success is having to worry about every damn thing in the world except money."

# CHAPTER 26: THE BIGGEST HURDLE

Of all the chapters in this book, this one is probably the most important. What I have found through my real estate journey is "How" is not the biggest hurdle to overcome. How do I purchase my first rental property? How do I get a loan? How do I get a quality tenant? "How" is a question best left for the experts. And those experts are my team. They provided all the answers to "How". People love to share their experiences and knowledge and my team is no different. Only a few phone calls to my local bank manager and real estate agent led to the organic formation of the rest of my team. And then, I realized "how" would come just as naturally and organically as my team.

I would like to share with you the truly biggest hurdle that prevents us from taking the next step, from creating change in our daily behaviors, and from pushing outside of our own boundaries. It is the hurdle of our own mind's doubts. Each step I have taken on my journey with real estate investments has pushed me out of my comfort zone and I have had my share of doubts along the way. How I approached this hurdle has made all the difference.

To overcome my own mind's doubts required a commitment to training my mind to think differently. To do this, I continually remind myself that there are literally millions of people in the world who are doing what I want to do. They are buying and building businesses, investing in real estate, and becoming millionaires. So that proves that it is not impossible. It is only a matter of changing my own behaviors and actions to emulate what they are doing. I have come to realize there is no need to feel hurried or to feel I have missed the party. There will always be new ideas, new opportunities and properties to invest. Every time I have missed a real estate deal, a new one soon came along. When I look at the time and work it takes to purchase a property, I remind myself that it is only a few months of work for a life time of returns! I remind myself of the countless hours needed at a 9-5 job to make a reasonable amount of money and then afterwards, to continue making that money, you have to do the same work again and again. A 9-5 job is truly trading your life for money!

I have a list of my favorite quotes. I reread them time to time to strengthen my resolve. Here are some of my favorites:

> "Make the most of yourself, for that
> is all there is of you."
> -Ralph Waldo Emerson

> "What lies behind us and what lies
> before us are tiny matters compared
> to what lies within us."
> -Ralph Waldo Emerson

"Success is the sum of small efforts,
repeated day in and day out"
-Robert Collier

"Life's not about how hard of a hit
you can give… it's about how many
you can take, and still keep moving
forward."

-Sylvester Stallone, Rocky "Do not
wait until conditions are perfect to
begin. Beginning makes the conditions perfect."
-Alan Cohen

"Courage is resistance to fear, mas-
tery of fear, not absence of fear."
-Mark Twain

"What you get by achieving your
goals is not as important as what you
become by achieving your goals.
-Henry David Thoreau

"Don't let life discourage you; everyone who got where he is had to begin
where he was."
-Richard L. Evans


And when I am scared of what could go wrong,
what could happen if I have a bad deal, a bad tenant,

or if I make a mistake, I remind myself, that I am not gambling. I am making logical decisions based on the years of experience of my team. And in life, nothing is guaranteed. Something could potentially go wrong. But I am going to live my life to the fullest! Failure is a part of life and if I fail, I'm going to fail going after something big. I would much prefer that, then the regret of spending years of my life at a 9-5 job. Life has its ups and downs but it's those ups and downs that feels like life!

# CHAPTER 27: PLANS AND BACKUP PLANS

I have always had back up plans in place. My first question when I make an investment, is if this investment is a flop what is the worst that could happen, and how would I need to respond? If the numbers make sense and I can live with the answers to those two questions, I make the investment.

It is important to point out that real estate is not gambling. I never "take a chance" on a property. I know ahead of time if a property is going to be profitable because I do my homework. I sit down with a pencil, paper, and a calculator and I assess a property from every angle to determine what my numbers are going to look like. I speak with my team. I speak with my mortgage lender to determine rate, an insurance broker to determine insurance prices and my realtor to calculate property values and help me make an offer. My realtor has also been instrumental in helping me determine estimated costs of needed repairs and likely rental rates for particular properties. It is only when the numbers make sense that I make the investment.

Even though I crunch the numbers ahead of time, no one can predict the future. I always have a back-up plan in place. When using other people's money to invest it is wise to have multiple options to pay back those funds if an investment does not work out as planned.

In my situation, due to the strong financial foundation we have set for ourselves, if it takes longer than expected to get a tenant if absolutely needed I could utilize profit from another property. Or if needed, I can draw from my 401k (with penalty). Another option I have available is to draw from my roth IRA if there were a dire need. And now that I have paid back my HELOC loan, I could obtain another HELOC if needed. In fact, I have multiple properties that I could obtain a HELOC.

Ever since college I have had a back-up plan in place. I went to college and developed a career not as just my primary goal. It was a career I love and enjoy, and it was something I could do until I was wealthy. With my career, I could support my family and meet my financial obligations as I went for true wealth.

# CHAPTER 28: REPAIRS AND UNEXPECTED EXPENSES

I delved into real estate to improve my financial situation and to make my life easier…not harder. When there is a broken toilet, a leak in the roof, or another unexpected issue with a house, I turn to my team. If my tenant calls me and says that a toilet is not working I inform them that I will get someone out there right away. I call my plumber, give him the tenant's phone number, and then I have the plumber send me the bill. My end of the work is then over.

Some landlords will try to save $100. It would involve driving to the house, evaluating the problem, traveling to the hardware store, driving back to the house and then repairing the problem. That is not my idea of fun! And I am not a plumber or a handyman by any stretch of the imagination. When I send my plumber out, I know the needed repairs will be done right, will be done fast, and the tenant will be happy. Pay the money. Remember, it is time to think of money differently. You are perhaps purchasing

$100,000 houses. If you can do that, you can learn the benefit of paying

$100 or more for a repair. Real estate needs to be thought of as a business. It is expected that there are expenses with a business. Do not let these small amounts take away from the big picture.

The real money is made with large transactions and repeated transactions such as the monthly rental payment. Once you become accustomed in dealing with the larger amounts of money dictated by real estate expenditures, $100 or more for a repair is worth the time and frustration it saves you.

# CHAPTER 29: YOU GET WHAT YOU PAY FOR

It can be tempting to attempt to save money and not use professionals. But when it comes to your main support team including your realtor and accountant their fees are well earned. Remember, they are the rocket engineers. Some people attempt to buy or sell real estate without a realtor to save money. I highly advise against this. If you are buying real estate, the seller is the one who pays for the realtor. And if you are selling real estate, a realtor can help you obtain top dollar, avoid paperwork mistakes, avoid legal mistakes, and make your life easier. Are you seeing a trend? Real estate investing is not meant to make your life harder. It is meant to make your life easier. A good high producing realtor can offer a wealth of information and knowledge. They are the consultant that is ready to answer your questions. I could not be where I am today without my realtor.

An accountant is a licensed professional that also can offer a wealth of information. If you do not currently have an accountant, get one. I advise, next time you need your taxes done, get a certified public accountant to do your taxes. This will give you the information you need to better understand the tax impact real estate investments will have for you. An accountant will charge you a fee for their services, but it is well worth it. They can help you avoid tax pitfalls and get the most back from your tax returns.

The same can be said with other team members as well. Having an experienced inspector to evaluate a home prior to purchasing it can help you avoid a costly mistake. Spending four or five hundred dollars for an inspection on a house you end up not buying is better than spending tens of thousands of dollars on a house you do buy because you did not have an inspector.

# CHAPTER 30: STAYING ORGANIZED

Staying organized is key especially when investing in multiple properties. I have a binder for each property. As bills or statements come in for properties, they are immediately filed into their respective binder. Each one has sections labeled mortgage papers, escrow account, property taxes, purchase agreement, initial inspection, insurance, flood insurance, previous tenant, current tenant, and receipts.

I also keep a spreadsheet for each property. It can be difficult to see the true returns real estate brings, other than the immediate cash flow. Much of the returns is in the form of principle payments and appreciation. In each spreadsheet, I track the rental income each month, the expenditures each month including the mortgage payment, the estimated value of the property, the amount owed, and the principle within the property. Every month when I receive a statement, I update these numbers.

By seeing the principle in each property, it makes it easier to creatively finance. I can easily see which properties I can take out a HELOC loan or perhaps do a cash out refinancing to purchase yet another property.

This also maintains motivation. Other than the monthly cash flow it can be difficult to appreciate the increase in net worth that occurs every month with principle payments and property appreciation. By having a spreadsheet and seeing the value of the property listed versus what is owed it can illuminate just how much real estate is increasing your net worth. Below is an example of my first five properties at a moment in time. The left column shows the full monthly payment on the property, the middle column shows the interest (which is tax deductible) and the third column shows the principle being paid down every month. Below the table are the totals for the 5 properties for a month period of time.

| Full Payment | Interest | Principle |
|---|---|---|
| 1,344.06 | 464.00 | 615.00 |
| 1,123.35 | 391.00 | 514.00 |
| 1,157.99 | 467.00 | 488.00 |
| 660.00 | 291.00 | 147.00 |
| 893.37 | 467.00 | 167.00 |

As you can see, for all five of the properties, $1,931 is being paid toward the principle every month. As the mortgage payments continue over time the percentage of the payment that goes to principle increases every month. This chart also does not take into consideration that the properties will increase in value further increasing the principle in the property. And with current tax laws, the interest portions of the payments can be deducted at the end of the year.

Each property also has its own separate spread sheet. Here you can see a spreadsheet for one of my properties with January through April payments and mortgages during 2021. The monthly rent is $1950 but a few of the payments are higher due to late fees paid by the tenant. The mortgage payments are listed on the right column. Every month, as I input the deposits and mortgage payments, the spreadsheet automatically updates the total deposits and total payments. Below it subtracts any maintenance costs leaving the year to date profit at the bottom.

| Date | Rent Deposits | Mortgage Payments | Date | Escrow Refunds |
|---|---|---|---|---|
| January | 1,950.00 | (888.42) | | |
| February | 2,000.00 | (893.37) | | |
| March | 2,020.00 | (893.37) | | |
| April | 1,950.00 | (893.37) | | |
| May | | | | |
| June | | | | |
| July | | | | |
| August | | | | |
| September | | | | |
| October | | | | |
| November | | | | |
| December | | | | |
| | 7,920.00 | (3,568.53) | | 0.00 |

Flood Insurance
Date paid

Maintenance Costs Total: ($300.00)

| | |
|---|---|
| Total Debits | (3,868.53) |
| Total Credits | 7,920.00 |
| PROFIT | 4,051.47 |

Once the spreadsheet has been set up, the rest is easy. Every month I sit at the computer and enter in the rental deposits, mortgage payments, maintenance fees, flood insurance payments and any mileage required for the properties. The spreadsheets do the calculations for me. The spreadsheets provide me an up to date "snap shot" of my total real estate picture.

# CHAPTER 31: VACATION HOME

Since I was a kid, I have always dreamed of a home in the mountains. As I grew older, my dreams grew into an obsession. I would have a home in the mountains! I spent many hours on the internet looking at mountain towns, log homes, and vacant land. Before I even had an idea how I could possibly afford a mountain home, I knew just how it would look.

I had my first five investment properties, my net worth improved substantially, and I was seeing monthly income. Could I be ready for my mountain home? I remembered the lesson from Robert Kiyosaki's book, "Rich Dad, Poor Dad". The rich don't say "I can't afford that. They say, "How can I afford that." At this point I had been accustomed to pushing my boundaries, but this was different. I knew mountain homes did not come cheap.

On a prior vacation to Colorado, I found a mountainside, with homes overlooking Rocky Mountain National Park. It was an amazing location. I happened to see a realtor sign at the base of that mountain so I jotted down the phone number. I kept that number with me for several months after that vacation. Occasionally, I would talk to my wife about my desire to buy a mountain home. Well…it wasn't occasionally. I was obsessed with the idea and it was difficult to think of anything else. One day, I decided I would stop dreaming and go for it. I called the number of the realtor I jotted down months before. At the time, I had no idea he would be my next team member. It was his knowledge and experience that helped carry me to the next level in real estate. He happened to own a vacation property rental management company on the mountain. This could be my answer to "How can I afford it?" If I could rent a vacation home when I wasn't using it, I could use that income to pay for my expenses. He invited me to come look at some properties for sale on the mountain.

I immediately said I would come meet him, I would just need to find some plane tickets first. I was amazed at what I then realized. I didn't think twice about traveling one thousand miles to meet with a realtor for one day. I didn't think twice about the costs of the plane ticket. I had changed. Every step of my journey, I was becoming more and more confident. I was not the same person that was shaking like a leaf on the inside prior to purchasing my first investment property. I knew what I was doing because I had done it before.

On the plane ride there I felt something wonderful. I felt like I was truly living. I was doing big things and my doubts were much more easily cast aside then they would have been eight years earlier. When I arrived, I met the realtor at a breakfast diner. As we talked, I realized he was me in the future. He had a mountain property on that very mountain. He was someone initially who lived far away and accomplished his dream of living in the mountains. He was another rocket engineer for the rocket I wanted to build, and he was ecstatic to share his knowledge for someone else on the same journey.

I lay everything out on the table before him. I told him my dream to have a home in the mountains. I explained my financial situation. I discussed my experience in real estate. He told me about his company and how he could help me reach my dream.

After breakfast, we went up the mountain. He showed me vacant land, condo homes, and million dollar estates. The view was breathtaking. I told him, "I want to be on this mountain. I will figure out a way to be on this mountain." The next day, I caught my flight back home. I knew I had some strategizing (and some math) to do.

Over the next few months, he emailed me some properties for sale on the mountain. And then one day, he sent me one in particular that just felt right. It was one half of a duplex condo. It had a large beautiful deck with a hot tub and it overlooked the main mountain range. It was 3 bedroom, 2 bath. It was bordered by Roosevelt National Forest a short distance above the property line. Even more appealing, Rocky Mountain National Park was within a short walk down the road to the South of the property. It was for sale for $560,000.

I knew that this was the one. The only problem was that real estate in the area was selling at a premium and was selling fast. Properties were being sold at asking price and were being sold sight unseen. But I had a team member there that I trusted. I spent several days looking at my options to purchase the property. He introduced me to a Colorado licensed mortgage broker named Rich and Rich was familiar not only with the area, but also vacation rental management programs in the area including the realtor's rental program. The information provided by Rich (the broker) and my realtor (the owner of the vacation property rental management company) was essential, to qualify for the loan. I would need to show that a substantial portion of the mortgage would be covered by the rental income that the property could generate. For several days, my kitchen table was littered with math scribbled papers, notes from numerous phone calls to insurance agents, Colorado housing inspectors, and calls to the mortgage lender, Rich.

After lots of math, I had my plan, I would take a secured loan against my stocks to cover a 20% down payment, and the remaining would be financed with a 30 year fixed rate mortgage. I would be zero dollars out of pocket for the initial purchase, and I would enter the property into the realtor's vacation rental management program to support the mortgage. I would also utilize some of the cash flow from my other investment properties as needed to pay down the mortgage.

This property would give me my vacation home. I would have a place my family and I could visit every year and call our own. I would also have control over a $560,000 property which would be financed with today's dollars. If it appreciates at the average 3% per year of a typical property, I would gain $16,800 in equity every year in addition to the $5,500 in principle I would be paying yearly during the beginning of the loan giving me a total of $22,300 equity per year. My plan also considered that rental rates for the property would likely go up with time increasing the amount of the mortgage covered by the vacation rental program.

I was ready to make the deal. I contacted my realtor and had him put in my offer to purchase the property at asking price. The sellers accepted.

After that, day by day, I waited to sign the contract. But something was changing. I was becoming unsure of my decision. I had worked so hard to get where I was that I was fearful of pushing myself too far, and everything could come crashing down. I was afraid of failure. My worries grew until I became scared. I emailed my Colorado realtor and told him I was having second thoughts. I even questioned if it were too late to get out of the contract.

Later that day, I received a response from my realtor. Here are some excerpts from his email.

"Before you pull the red and white striped handle, please consider this: I have never known one single person who 'regretted' buying or building a home here. Stressful? Oh yeah. Sleepless nights? Guaranteed. Consternation and concern. Uh-huh. But no one I know has regretted what they DID nearly as much as those who have come to regret what they didn't do when they had the chance."

"I cannot make this decision for you and your wife. But I will tell you, if you weren't stressed, you probably bought too small a home. Everyone who buys up here stresses. At every level, earning level and age group, it's stressfully expensive. It. Just. Is."

These were the words that made all the difference. A member of my team came through for me and helped me see that what I was feeling was normal...even expected. I realized at that time, that my own fears had withered my resolve. When the time came to push my boundaries and go for what I wanted, I instead was about to back out. I almost set myself up for a life time of "what if's?" and regret.

I decided at that time, I would go through with the deal. It was something I wanted, and it was time to go big. It was over a half million- dollar piece of property, but I was the person who had five investment properties. I was the person who had a team. I was the person that pushed his own boundaries. I purchased the property, and it felt like living! Today, that property that I almost didn't purchase is worth $880,000 with much of the mortgage covered by the short term rentals from the vacation home rental program.

# CHAPTER 32: WHAT IS WEALTH

On our journey to wealth, a very simple question that is paramount to the goal if often overlooked. "What is wealth?" Is it a million dollars? It is ten million dollars? Is it a six or seven figure income? Is it investment properties?

In my own mind I have developed a definition of wealth. It is the point in which I no longer have to trade my time for money. It is when I no longer have to choose between spending time with my family versus spending time away from my family to earn money for my family.

So how can we find out when we are wealthy? We need to ask ourselves, "At what point do we have more money coming in from investments, royalties, and other passive income then we have going out? When is our cash flow positive without having to trade our time and effort for money? To find the answer to this we need to know how much money is flowing out which can be based on monthly or yearly cash flow.

For this example, we will consider yearly cash flow and we will use a few tried and true assumptions. We will assume we can withdraw 4% yearly on any investments such as a 401k, roth ira, or stocks. We will next determine how much yearly income we need in retirement. Most people use the assumption of 75% to 80% of current income yearly, because we will not likely to have a mortgage or dependents in retirement. But we are not most people. We are planning to be rich in retirement! So let's start with an even number that is substantial enough to provide a very easy retirement for most people without having to work... let's say ($200,000) per year. If we are drawing 4% on retirement savings, that would mean we need

$5,000,000 saved for retirement. If that is a goal you decide to set for yourself, then you will need to find a way to draw 4% off of any savings yearly plus cash flow from investments, royalties, or passive income to equal $200,000 per year cash flow.

With real estate investments, positive cash flow from monthly rental income substantially decreases the amount of savings needed to attain your goal. If you start early enough, many of the mortgages on the properties may even be paid off further increasing the amount of monthly income from each property. But then again, these properties, could be cash out refinanced, to purchase additional properties to provide even more positive cash flow for retirement!

So when can you retire? So when should you retire? Both of these questions are personal and no one can answer them for you. Many people have careers or jobs that they truly love. For these people, these careers may be how they want to spend their days. But then there are other people who do not like their day jobs and they continue to trade their time and lives for money.

For both groups of people, I pose the question, "Do you HAVE to work?". Do your financial responsibilities demand that you put in 40 hours per week to meet those obligations? Whether or not you love your job, HAVING to do something to meet all of your obligations including daily expenses, paying debts, and supporting your family, can be quite stressful and is not a secure position to be in. If there is one constant in this world, it is change. Companies go bankrupt, companies can downsize, or be bought by a conglomerate, or leadership can change. Your security is at the whims of any one of these events that can and do happen.

How much better would it be to have passive income? For those that love what they do, how great would it be to do what you love everyday not because you HAVE to, but because you want to do it?

We all hear in the news that people are living longer. And with this change, retirement ages are also creeping up. A standard retirement used to be 65 but more and more people are retiring at 68, 70, or never retiring! The older we live, the longer our money has to last. One way people accomplish this is to work longer.

However; as we progress as a society, we should be retiring younger, not older! It is difficult for most any savings to last from age 55 to 80. But what if instead, passive income from cash flow came in every month. Then it would not be necessary to have a huge savings account to retire at 55. Instead, if the cash flow being produced is greater than the cash flow going out, then you have a level of wealth in which you do not HAVE to work anymore.

# CHAPTER 33: BEING FEARFUL IS OK

If you are reading this book, you undoubtedly have an interest in investing in real estate. Perhaps you are reading this book for the initial steps I listed for purchasing my first rental properties, or perhaps you are looking to motivate yourself to make the leap into real estate. If you are anything like me, you may be fearful about the adventure in which you considering embarking.

It is ok to be fearful. Do not let fear of change make you feel weak or unsure of yourself. After all, being brave has nothing to do with not being afraid. Being brave is acting despite the fear! And it is that action in which you will show your true strength.

After the first rental property is purchased and you have collected a rent check or two, your level of fear will be greatly reduced and will be replaced with confidence. You will look back and admire your own strength as you acted despite your own mind's hurdles. You will have started to succeed!

There have been multiple times when I have been fearful. There were ways during my journey that I overcame my own mind's hurdle of fear. Initially, the first way I controlled my fear was to strengthen my resolve with my own mind. I needed to dig deep to determine what I really wanted and tap my inner passion. I knew that I really wanted to be rich! Some days my fear was at a minimum and other days my fears hurt my confidence. But my passion kept me going. I would exercise my mind by reading my favorite motivational quotes, reading articles and blogs of those that reached the same success wanted, and I still maintained the strength to picture myself living the life I knew I would have. Exercising my own mind was perhaps the hardest way to control my fears, but is was also the most important and necessary way in the beginning.

Eventually, the second way I controlled my fears was to have a team. They brought their expertise and years of experience to the table. They took the 'How' out of the equation and helped to remove that fear. I had confidence in my team which removed many of my worries.

My team's experience is still paramount to my investments and I rely on their knowledge, but now my fears have made way for my own experience.

With each property I purchase, I know I have done it before and can do it again. As the process becomes more and more automatic, any hurdles that arise, appear less problematic. I no longer have to rely as much on resolve and my team overcome my fears as now I have my own innate confidence!

# CHAPTER 34: THE NINE STEPS SUMMARIZED

In the beginning of this book, I discussed my first nine steps into real estate. Here I will list those steps and then I will summarize each.

1.  Introduced to Rich Dad,Poor Dad book
2.  Having a smart financial start
3.  First rental house
4.  Failure
5.  Partnering with my wife
6.  A short drive to the bank
7.  Obtaining a HELOC
8.  Purchasing the first property
9.  Rinse, wash, repeat

Step number 1- Introduced to Rich Dad, Poor Dad book.

I consider this book my first step into real estate. It was not only my motivation to push my boundaries, but it was also a window into a world I could not have otherwise easily seen. Education is one of the strongest assets we can have in life. With new knowledge, our mind can become open to things we never before knew existed. Our minds are incredible machines that allow us to react to environmental cues. With education, we are constantly enriching our mind, and education needs to be a lifelong endeavor especially in a world changing so quickly. Without the input of new knowledge, our mind will not react differently than it has before. Read everything you can to further your knowledge of real estate. Speak with your team, get their thoughts, and use their wisdom.

Step number 2- Having a smart financial start.

Without a strong financial start, I will have still found a way to invest in real estate. But it would have been more difficult and possibly progressed slower in the beginning. Perhaps the easiest way to insure a smart financial start is to live below your means. My wife and I could have enjoyed a much higher standard of living in our early years, but we understood delayed gratification. We lived off of the lower salary, bought generic, took advantage of sales, and then bought only a small house. While it is true that you do not need money to make money, having money sure makes it a lot easier.

Step number 3- First rental house.

My situation presented me with an unusual opportunity. Because I was unable to sell my first house, I decided to rent it. This introduced me to investment management companies, lease contracts, and tax implications of investment properties. It also allowed me to see that real estate could truly increase my net worth and was a viable investment option. It also was a source of pride to know that I had a second property.

Step number 4- Failure.

I site failure as a step because it was paramount. I learned and I let that failure become an important part of myself. When not used to its full potential, failure can lead to depression, weakness and defeat. But, instead, flip the script, and then failure can become a great strength. My business did not get off to the start I had hoped. I could have accepted my failure and not made a change. But fortunately, my failure was the fuel to my drive. Without failure, I would not be the person I am today. It is important to expect to fail on the road to success. Why do we think that we would be perfect when doing something we have never done. Fail, fail again, and fail often to learn and succeed.

Step number 5- Partnering with my spouse.

Being married introduces a whole other aspect to investing in real estate. With any investment there is risk, and that risk can affect the spouse. It is important to discuss each other's financial goals and risk tolerance to have a better understanding of each other's viewpoint. For some relationships, real estate investing may not be the best option. For others, it could be challenge that can become a shared goal and strengthen the bond.

Step number 6- A short drive to the bank.

To begin my fact finding, my first task was to speak with a bank manager about getting a loan. This was one of the most important steps that I had taken. I felt a surge in confidence as I drove to the bank. It was a moment of action! I was really doing it! I was taking a step to become a real estate investor. It wasn't talk, it wasn't thinking, and it wasn't a long drawn out journey. It was a quick concrete action. I was driving to a bank, but in reality, I was also driving toward my future!

Step number 7- Obtaining a HELOC.

My path to investment properties began with a home equity line of credit (HELOC) loan. It was an interest only loan where I could pay the principle down at my leisure. The down payments and repairs for my first three investment properties were funded with this HELOC loan. I was using other people's money to provide my cash flow and increase in net worth. All three of my first properties were funded completely through the HELOC and thirty-year mortgages.

Step number 8- Purchasing the first property.

Making the leap and purchasing my first property intended as an investment was a huge hurdle. I had a team and I did the math, but it still required an effort to overcome my fears. From the moment I told Scott I wanted to purchase the property, I felt like I was accomplishing something. I also felt like everything could go wrong. I did not have the confidence yet to feel assured I was making the right decision. But I couldn't have the confidence at this point, because I had never done something like that before. But I did overcome my fears and had the bravery to act.

Step number 9- Rinse, wash, repeat.

Why stop purchasing real estate? I made the mistake of being comfortable and content for a two-year period of time between property purchases. Once you have purchased a rental property, it only becomes easier. Each property purchased opens up different avenues for further investments. Net worth increases, cash flow increases, and your experience increases. As you develop your team, your support strengthens. You may need to pursue more creative financing but at this point you have the know-how and the confidence.

# CHAPTER 35: YOUR FIRST STEP

Your first step into real estate may not be the same as mine if you even decide real estate is for you. I have offered you a window into my actions taken for my first five houses. I have laid out my fears, hesitations, and mistakes to let you know that you are not alone with these thoughts. I provided a look into the thought processes that go along with pushing boundaries, because I did not have that benefit. I laid out the steps and hurdles I faced as a source I wish I had when I first started real estate. I did not know if what I was thinking through the beginning of my real estate venture was typical. I did not know if my hesitations and fears were due to weakness or were normal. I wish I could go back in time to remind myself, that hesitations and fear were normal. And because of those hurdles, I was able to find strength in myself. I was able to take concrete actions in my life to make a change. I began by reading a book on real estate, and I acted upon it. Perhaps this book may serve as step one for someone. If so, find a way to quickly make it to step 6- A quick drive to the bank. It is a concrete action and perhaps the best way to discover what options are available to you to overcome the "how" of investing in real estate.

And overcoming the mental hurdles along the way will be up to you. It takes a deep passion for someone to maintain motivation and even then, its only natural that motivation may wax and wane. Exercise your mind routinely to control your fears as you begin your journey. It takes effort to strengthen your resolve. As you can see, you are not alone in any hurdles you place before yourself in your own mind. But be brave, and act despite the fear. When you do, it will feel like living!